An Introduction to Sports Science in English

英語で学ぶスポーツ科学

Julyan Nutt
Yoko Kurahashi
Shin Yamamoto

NAN'UN-DO

An Introduction to Sports Science in English

Download Audio

音声ファイル
無料 DL
のご案内

このテキストの音声を無料で視聴（ストリーミング）・ダウンロードできます。自習用音声としてご活用ください。
以下のサイトにアクセスしてテキスト番号で検索してください。

https://nanun-do.com　テキスト番号［**512182**］

※ 無線 LAN（WiFi）に接続してのご利用を推奨いたします。
※ 音声ダウンロードは Zip ファイルでの提供になります。
お使いの機器によっては別途ソフトウェア（アプリケーション）の導入が必要となります。

Read by
Shizuka Anderson
Kyle Card

※ An Introcuction to Sports Science in English 音声ダウンロードページは以下の QR コードからもご利用になれます。

はじめに

今日、大学生の英語力の多様化に伴い、到達度別の英語の教科書が多数出版されております。その一方で高等学校での教科書とは異なる内容も求められています。大学生の興味に合い、知性を刺激し、多様な英語レベルの学生に対応した教科書が理想と言えます。

本書はそのような教科書を目標にして作成しました。内容としては身体･スポーツ･健康（医療）等に関連する学部学生の専門に対応しておりますが、近年スポーツ・健康への関心が高いことから、これらを専門としない学生も興味をもって読むことができるよう配慮してあります。教科書のレベルは中級程度ですが､初級でも対応できるよう注も豊富につけてあります。本書は読解・語彙・文法・作文・リスニングの力を高めるための豊富な練習問題も準備した総合教材です。

本書の具体的な特徴は以下の通りです。

1. 読解のためのパッセージは 250 語前後と 130 語前後の 2 つあり､読みやすくしてあります。
2. パッセージの内容理解のための練習問題があります。
3. 専門用語を定着できるように工夫した練習問題があります。また、語彙力を増すために、派生語に注目した問題もあります。
4. リスニング力を強化するために、パッセージの内容に関連した練習問題があります。
5. パッセージで使用された構文や文法に焦点をおいた語の並べ替え問題があり、作文力も身につけることができます。

本書を通して英語の総合力を高めつつ、スポーツ・健康等について楽しく学ぶことを期待しております。

2023 年 1 月

筆者

本書の使い方

本書は、15ユニットから構成され、1～14の各ユニットは**Vocabulary**、**Passage 1**、**Comprehension check I・II**、**Passage 2**、**Comprehension check**、**Derivatives**、**Rearranging**から成り立っています。ユニット15は、復習のためのものです。

Vocabularyでは、**Passage 1**を読解するのに必要な単語を事前学習します。

Passage 1では、スポーツ科学に関連した英文を読み、英語の読解力を高めます。

Comprehension check Iでは、**Passage 1**の内容理解を英語で書かれたTrue/False Questionで確認します。

Comprehension check IIは、**Passage 1**の内容を要約した英文の空欄に専門用語を記入して文を完成し、専門用語の把握と内容理解を確認します。

Passage 2では、スポーツ関連の短いエッセーを英語で読み、英語の読解力を高めます。

Comprehension checkでは、音声を聞き、**Passage 2**に関する質問に対する解答文の空欄に入る単語を書き取り、リスニング力を高めます。

Derivativesでは、**Passage 1**と**Passage 2**で使用された単語の派生語（動詞／名詞）の練習問題を通して派生語のパターンを理解します。

Rearrangingでは、**Passage 1**と**Passage 2**に出てくる構文や文法を使用した英文を作るために、日本語の意味になるように単語を並べ替え、英作文力を高めます。

上記を行うことで、スポーツやスポーツ科学の知識を英語で学びつつ、英語の読解力、語彙力、文法、リスニング力等の英語の総合力を高めます。

Contents

Unit 1
Introduction to Sports Science
スポーツ科学への序説

Vocabulary

次の単語の意味を a ～ e の中から選びなさい。

1. physical fitness (　)　2. physiology (　)　3. psychology (　)
4. nutrition (　)　5. physiotherapist (　)

a. 心理学　b. 栄養　c. 理学療法士　d. 体の健康、体力　e. 生理学

Passage 1

02

Since the birth of the Olympics in Ancient Greece, athletes have tried to get a **competitive advantage** over each other. However, it was not until later that the **principles** of science were applied to sport. After the Second World War there was a battle between two global powers: the United States of America and the Soviet Union (what we now think of as Russia). There was a nuclear arms race, a race to put the first person on the moon, and a race to produce the greatest athletes. At that time the Soviet Union encouraged physical fitness, and supported scientific research into this **field**. Once the USA realized that Russian athletes had a competitive advantage, they also started sports science research.

There are three main scientific fields in sports science: physiology, **biomechanics**, and psychology. Physiology uses **biological** principles to study how the body reacts to exercise and training. Biomechanics uses **mechanical** principles to study how the body moves and reacts to equipment. Psychology uses **psychological** principles to study human **behavior**.

The field of sports science is always growing. The importance of nutrition in improving athletic **performance** is now understood. The relationship between physical activity and health is also applied to our everyday lives. **Motor control**–the role of the brain in movement–is now better understood. The role sport plays in society is studied in **sport sociology**.

As the science of sport has grown, so have the career-related fields. Athletes require managers, coaches, **nutritionists**, and physiotherapists. The general public also uses personal trainers and health supplements. And with all the money in the **global industry** of sport, more money can be invested in scientific research to improve athletic performance even more.

注　**competitive advantage**「競争上の優位性」　**principles**「原理」　**field**「分野」　**biomechanics**「バイオメカニクス、生体（生物）力学」　**biological**「生物学の」　**mechanical**「力学的な」　**psychological**「心理学の」　**behavior**「行動」　**performance**「出来栄え、パフォーマンス」**motor control**「運動制御」　**sport sociology**「スポーツ社会学」　**nutritionist**「栄養士」　**global industry**「世界的産業」

Comprehension check

I. 次の英文が Passage 1 の内容と一致しているなら T (true) を、一致していないなら F (false) を（　）内に記入しなさい。

1. The principles of science have been applied to sport since the birth of the Olympics in Ancient Greece.　(　　)
2. The Soviet Union encouraged physical fitness after the Second World War.　(　　)
3. Biomechanics, the study of the body's movement, is one of three main scientific fields in sports science.　(　　)
4. In sport sociology the relationship between physical activity and society is studied.　(　　)
5. Because there is so much money in the global industry of sport, more money can be invested in sport science.　(　　)

II. 次の英文が Passage 1 の内容と一致するように下記の語群から適切なものを選択し、空欄に記号を記入しなさい。

1. Trying to get a (　　) has not changed since the birth of sport.
2. After the Second World War, the USA realized Russian athletes had a competitive advantage and began (　　) research.
3. Biomechanics relates to the (　　) forces behind the motion of bodies.
4. It is common knowledge that nutrition is important to help improve (　　).
5. Nowadays there are managers, coaches, (　　), etc. behind professional athletes.

a. mechanical　　b. sports science　　c. athletic performance
d. competitive advantage　　e. physiotherapists

Passage 2 03

Leo Matveyev's theory of periodization

There have been many great Soviet sport scientists. One of the greatest is the physiologist, Leo Matveyev. He studied the performance of Soviet athletes in the 1952 and 1956 Olympics. After comparing the training schedules of successful athletes with unsuccessful athletes, he was able to create **periodized** training plans for the 1960 Rome Olympics. His plan was for the Soviet athletes to reach their peak performance at those Olympics. This was the height of the **Cold War**, so beating America had never been more important. The American track and field team was looking very strong. They had **dominated** most of the sporting competitions up until then. However, when the most important event, the Olympics, was held, they failed to dominate. They had peaked too soon. Even though the Soviet team had less talent, they were able to beat the Americans because of Matveyev's scientific training method.

注　**periodization**「期分け（試合にピークを合わせられるよう、トレーニング期間をいくつかの段階に分けること）」　**periodize**「期分けする」　**Cold War**「冷戦（第二次世界大戦後のアメリカ合衆国を中心とする西側諸国の 資本主義・自由主義陣営と、ソビエト連邦を中心とする東側諸国の共産主義・社会主義陣営との対立。）」　**dominate**「制覇する」

Comprehension check 04

音声を聞いて Passage 2 に関する質問への解答を空欄に３語記入して完成しなさい。

1. What did Leo Matveyev do?
   He (   ) comparing the training plans of successful athletes with unsuccessful ones.
2. What is the purpose of periodized training plans?
   It is that (   ) is achieved at the correct time.
3. Why did America fail to dominate at the 1960 Rome Olympics?
   Because (   ) the 1960 Rome Olympics.

Derivatives

次の表を完成しなさい。

Verb	Noun
	performance
	competition
fail	
periodize	
	movement

Rearranging

日本語の意味に合うように与えられた単語を使用して文を完成しなさい。文頭にくる語も小文字にしてある。

1. have, since, I, I, English, entered, studied
   中学校に入学以来、英語を勉強してきた。
   (　　　　　　　　　　　　　　　　　　　　) junior high school.
2. was, until, that, this, year, not
   今年になって初めて彼はその試合に勝った。
   It (　　　　　　　　　　　　　　　　　　　) he won the game.
3. accident, before, how, the, the, explained, happened, day
   彼はその事故が一昨日どのように起きたかを説明した。
   He (　　　　　　　　　　　　　　　　　　　　　) yesterday.
4. the, role, game, he, played, in, satisfied
   試合で彼の果たした役割は、ファンを満足させた。
   The (　　　　　　　　　　　　　　　　　　　　　) the fans.
5. as, her, English, she, improved, has
   彼女が英語を上達させたように、あなたも上達させた。
   (　　　　　　　　　　　　　　　　　　　　　　), so have you.

Unit 2

Physiology I: The Skeletal System

生理学 I—骨格組織

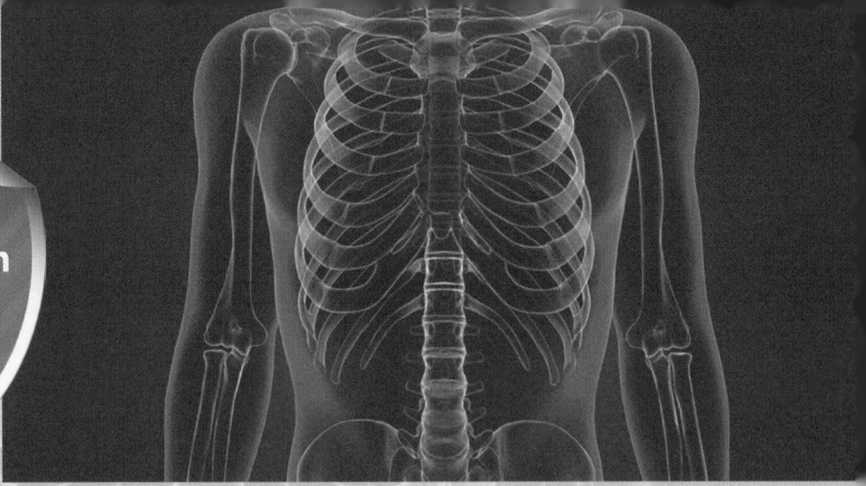

Vocabulary

次の単語の意味を a ～ e の中から選びなさい。

1. function ( )
2. force of gravity ( )
3. contract ( )
4. joint ( )
5. red blood cell ( )

a. 関節　b. 収縮　c. 赤血球　d. 機能　e. 重力

Passage 1

05

The **skeletal system** has three main functions: **support**, **attachment**, and **leverage**. Without the skeletal system the human body would be soft like a jellyfish and would not be able to stand up straight. Humans are **vertebrates**. This means they have a **spine**, or backbone. This is the central and most important bone in the skeletal system. The spine is made up of thirty-three small bones called **vertebrae**. The bones at the bottom of the spine are larger because they have to carry more weight. Those at the top of the spine are smaller and more flexible. They are used more for movement. The spine is curved, not straight. Being curved means that it can manage the force of gravity from above and **ground reaction forces** from below. When athletes run or jump, these ground reaction forces increase. Because the spine is complex, it can easily be injured. Although sport injuries to the spine are not the most common, they can often be the most serious and can end athletes' careers. Contact sports such as American football, ice hockey and wrestling are where spinal injuries happen most often.

Bones have places where muscles can attach. When the muscles contract, the bones move through joints. Longer bones act as **levers**, increasing the speed or force of the movement. We can see this when a soccer player takes a free kick, or when a baseball pitcher pitches a ball. The skeletal system also protects our organs: the skull protects the brain, and the **ribcage** protects the lungs and heart. Bones are strong, but they are flexible and not particularly heavy. Many people believe that the skeletal system is the heaviest part of the body, however this is not true. It is 10~15% of our total body weight. What else do bones do? They also store minerals and fats, and in some bones red blood cells are produced.

注 **skeletal system**「骨格組織」 **support**「支えること」 **attachment**「連結」 **leverage**「てこの作用」 **vertebrate**「脊椎動物（せきついどうぶつ）」 **spine**「脊椎骨」 **vertebra(e)**「脊椎（複数形は e をつける）」 **ground reaction force**「地面反力」 **lever**「てこ」 **ribcage**「胸郭」

Comprehension check

I. 次の英文が Passage 1 の内容と一致しているなら T (true) を、一致していないなら F (false) を（ ）内に記入しなさい。

1. With the skeletal system humans can stand up straight. ( )
2. The spine is straight and can manage the force of gravity from above. ( )
3. Spinal injuries happen so often that athletes should not do contacts sports. ( )
4. We cannot move our bones without the muscles, which are attached to our joints. ( )
5. The skeletal system's minerals protect the lungs and heart. ( )

II. 次の英文が Passage 1 の内容と一致するように下記の語群から適切なものを選択し、空欄に記号を記入しなさい。

1. Humans who have spines, or backbones, belong to ( ).
2. The larger bones of the ( ) at the bottom carry more weight than the top ones.
3. The spine is curved so that it can manage ( ) when people run or jump.
4. When a baseball pitcher throws a ball, he uses the longer forearm bone as a ( ).
5. The ( ) is 10~15% of our total body weight.

a. spine	b. ground reaction forces	c. skeletal system
d. vertebrates	e. lever	

Passage 2 06

Matthew Fraser: Weightlifter / CrossFit athlete

At 19 years old Matthew Fraser was training as an Olympic weightlifter. When he was doing a particularly heavy lift, he broke two vertebrae in his spine. His doctors told him that he would never lift again and, after four months of treatment, his spine still had not healed. His doctor recommended having the vertebrae **fused** together, but Matthew knew that this surgery would finish his sporting career. Instead, he decided to try a new type of surgery where he would have his back broken again, before being rejoined. That treatment only had a 50% chance of success. After four months Matthew was back training again. While still training as a weightlifter, Matthew started using a **CrossFit** gym because it has the same equipment as for weightlifting. Gradually, he became interested in CrossFit. Now, Matthew Fraser is known as one of the fittest men in the world, having won the CrossFit Games every time from 2016 to 2020.

注　**CrossFit**「クロスフィット（グレッグ・グラスマンにより 2000 年にアメリカで設立されたフィットネス団体）」　**fuse**「結合させる」

Comprehension check 07

音声を聞いて Passage 2 に関する質問への解答を空欄に３語記入して完成しなさい。

1. What happened when Matthew Fraser was attempting a heavy lift?
   He (   ) in his spine.
2. What did Matthew deicide?
   He decided he would have his (   ).
3. What is he famous for?
   He is famous for being one of (   ) in the world.

Derivatives

次の表を完成しなさい。

Verb	Noun
	weight
	treatment
	success
recommend	
	equipment

Rearranging

日本語の意味に合うように与えられた単語を使用して文を完成しなさい。文頭にくる語も小文字にしてある。

1. without, help, I, your, couldn't, finish
   君の助けがなかったら、仕事を終えることができなかった。
   ( ) my task.
2. woman, Lucy, me, a, telephoned, called
   ルーシーという女の人が今朝電話をかけてきた。
   ( ) this morning.
3. it, fine, out, going, like, is, don't, feel, I
   天気がいいけれど、出かける気にはならない。
   Although ( ).
4. in, I, childhood, where, to, live, used, my
   ここは子供時代に住んでいた所です。
   This is ( ).
5. else, like, to, you, what, would
   他に何が言いたいですか。
   ( ) say?

Unit 3

Physiology II: Muscle Fiber Types

生理学 II ー筋線維タイプ

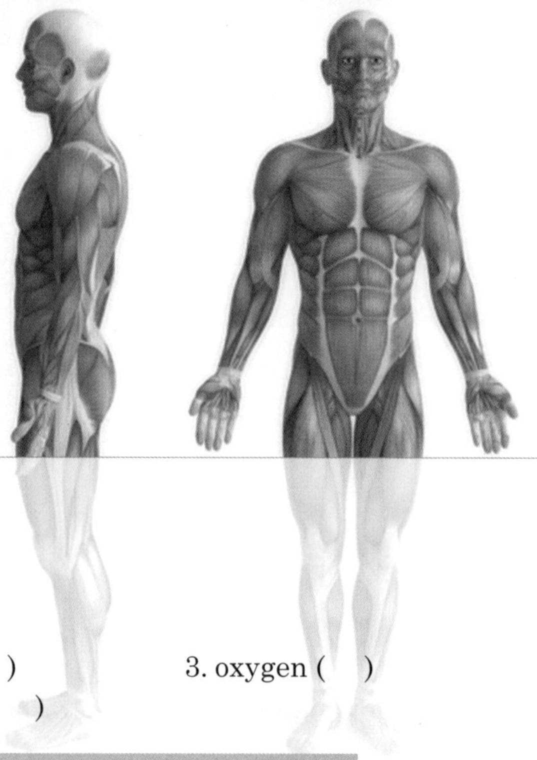

Vocabulary

次の単語の意味を a ～ e の中から選びなさい。

1. muscle (　)　　2. organ (　)　　3. oxygen (　)
4. recruit (　)　　5. produce (　)

a. 酸素　b. 用いる　c. 生み出す　d. 器官　e. 筋肉

Passage 1

08

Muscles have many functions. They are not only used for movement. The largest muscle in the human body helps us stand up straight, and the smallest muscle, in our ear, is needed for hearing. Muscles help us stay warm, and they also protect the organs in our body.

Muscles are made up of two types of **fiber**: slow twitch and fast **twitch**. Slow twitch fibers contract, or twitch, slowly and do not become tired easily. They are used for **endurance tasks**: that is tasks that happen over a long time. To do this they must have a good supply of oxygen, so they contain many **blood vessels** and a red-colored **protein** called **myoglobin**, which attracts oxygen. This gives slow twitch muscles their red color.

Fast twitch muscles are twice as big as slow twitch muscles, and they twitch twice as fast. Because they are bigger, they produce more force, so they are used for speed or power. However, fast twitch muscles tire easily because they get their energy **anaerobically**: without using much oxygen. Because they do not use much oxygen, they have fewer blood vessels and less myoglobin.

A muscle fiber is like an on/off switch: it is either contracted or not. For the fibers to contract, they need a signal from the brain. Different types of fibers need different signal strengths to contract. Slow twitch fibers will contract with a weak signal and fast twitch with a stronger signal. As the amount of force needed to complete a task increases, more and more fast twitch muscles will be recruited.

The human body is designed for both endurance and speed. A normal person has about 50% each of slow twitch and fast twitch fibers. However, endurance athletes such as marathon runners can have about 75% slow twitch muscles, and sprinters may have 75% fast twitch.

注　**fiber**「(筋) 線維」　**twitch**「攣縮（れんしゅく）、攣縮する」
endurance task「持久力タスク」　**blood vessel**「血管」
protein「タンパク質」　**myoglobin**「ミオグロビン」
anaerobically「嫌気的に（酸素の介在を伴わないで）」

Comprehension check

I. 次の英文が Passage 1 の内容と一致しているなら T (true) を、一致していないなら F (false) を（　）内に記入しなさい。

1. There is a muscle in our ear which helps move the organs in the ear.　(　　)
2. Slow twitch fibers contain many blood vessels and red-colored myoglobin.　(　　)
3. Fast twitch muscles contract twice as fast as slow twitch ones but have fewer blood vessels and less myoglobin.　(　　)
4. Muscle fibers contract according to a signal from the brain.　(　　)
5. It is not possible for someone to change the percentage of slow twitch and fast twitch fibers.　(　　)

II. 次の英文が Passage 1 の内容と一致するように下記の語群から適切なものを選択し、空欄に記号を記入しなさい。文頭にくる語も小文字にしてある。

1. Muscles are used for movement, standing up straight, hearing, staying warm, and (　　) in our body.
2. Slow twitch fibers are used (　　), and must have a good supply of oxygen.
3. Fast twitch muscles (　　) but tire more easily than slow twitch ones.
4. (　　) makes slow twitch fibers contract and a stronger signal fast twitch.
5. Marathon runners and sprinters can have about 75% slow twitch and 25% (　　) respectively.

a. fast twitch muscles	b. protecting the organs	c. produce more force
d. for endurance tasks	e. a weak signal	

Passage 2 09

What type of meat do you like?

Some people prefer the chicken breast, others the thigh. But is there a reason for this difference in taste and texture? The answer is, of course, yes. The chest muscles and leg muscles are used to do different jobs. Chickens stand or walk for most of the day, so the muscles in their legs are made up of **slow twitch fibers**. They contain myoglobin, which gives them the red color. The muscles on the chicken's chest are used to control their wings. Chickens can fly, but only for a short time. Flying requires a short burst of energy, so the chest muscles are made up of **fast twitch fibers**. Without the myoglobin, these muscles are white. And what about flavor? Chicken thighs are tastier because the slow twitch muscles contain more fat, which is used for energy.

注　**slow twitch fiber**「遅筋線維」　**fast twitch fiber**「速筋線維」

Comprehension check 10

音声を聞いて Passage 2 に関する質問への解答を空欄に３語記入して完成しなさい。

1. What are the muscles in the chicken thigh made of?
   They are made of (　　　　　　　　　　　　).
2. Why is chicken thigh tastier than breast?
   Because it (　　　　　　　　　　　　).
3. Why are slow twitch fibers red?
   Because (　　　　　　　　　　　　).

Derivatives

次の表を完成しなさい。

Verb	Noun
prefer	
require	
	endurance
need	
tire	

Rearranging

日本語の意味に合うように与えられた単語を使用して文を完成しなさい。文頭にくる語も小文字にしてある。

1. speak, dance, can, made, Japan, in, only, but, not
   この日本製のロボットは話すだけでなく踊ることができる。
   This robot (　　　　　　　　　　　　　　　　　　　　　　　　).
2. color, pale, called, in, yellow, the, the, picture
   私はその絵の中の淡黄色といわれる色が好きだ。
   I like (　　　　　　　　　　　　　　　　　　　　　　　　).
3. as, as, run, can, can, one, a, half, and, times, I, fast
   そのランナーは私の 1.5 倍速く走ることができる。
   The runner (　　　　　　　　　　　　　　　　　　　　　　　　).
4. and, as, grew, more, more, people, reputation, restaurant's, the
   そのレストランの評判が高まるにつれて、ますます人々はそこへ食事に行くようになった。
   (　　　　　　　　　　　　　　　　　　　　　　　　) went to eat there.
5. fruit, as, oranges, such, and, bananas, from, imports, Japan, fresh
   日本はオレンジやバナナのような生の果物を外国から輸入している。
   (　　　　　　　　　　　　　　　　　　　　　　　　) foreign countries.

Unit 4

Physiology III: The Cardio-Respiratory System

生理学 III ー心臓・呼吸器系

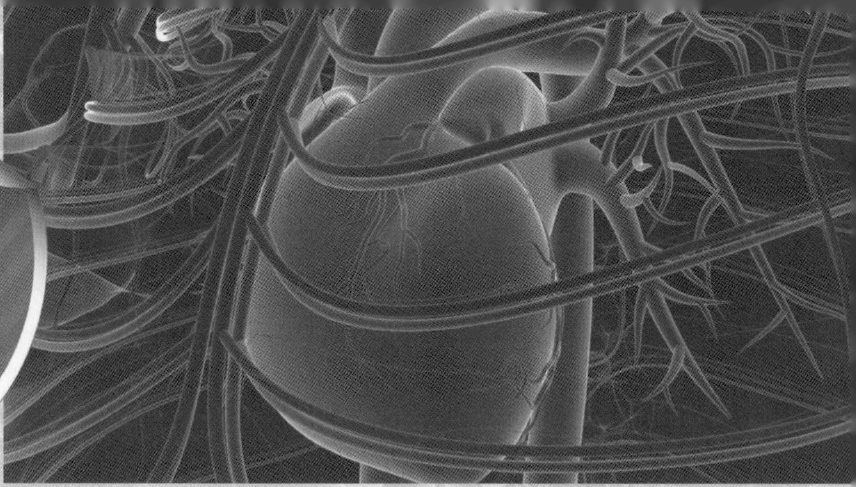

Vocabulary

次の単語の意味を a ～ e の中から選びなさい。

1. respiratory system (　)　　2. carbon dioxide (　)　　3. transport (　)
4. lactic acid (　)　　5. fatigue (　)

a. 運ぶ　b. 乳酸　c. 二酸化炭素　d. 疲労　e. 呼吸器系

Passage 1

11

Like all machines, our bodies need fuel to work. To do this the cells in our muscles need a constant supply of oxygen, **glucose** and **nutrients**. Oxygen is supplied to the blood through the respiratory system: breathing. Air passes through the nose or mouth to the lungs. Oxygen from the air enters the blood, and carbon dioxide is removed.

Oxygen, glucose and nutrients are then transported to the cells through the **cardiovascular system**. **Cardio** comes from the Greek word kardia meaning heart. **Vascular** means **vessels** that carry liquids–in this case blood. The heart pumps the blood through the blood vessels to the cells. The cardiovascular system also removes waste products, such as carbon dioxide and lactic acid, from the blood. The combination of these two systems is commonly known as the **cardio-respiratory system**.

Muscles need enough oxygen, glucose and other nutrients to work properly during high-intensity or long periods of exercise. If the muscles do not get enough nutrients, waste products increase and cause fatigue. The harder we exercise, the faster we breathe and the harder our hearts pump. More fuel (calories) is burned, more oxygen and nutrients are supplied to the muscles, and more waste products removed. The heart can be thought of as the engine that drives the system. A bigger engine releases more power. To this end, endurance athletes work hard to improve their cardio-respiratory system.

注　**glucose**「ブドウ糖」　**nutrient**「栄養物」　**cardiovascular system**「循環器系」　**cardio**「心臓」　**vascular**「導管（脈管・血管）の」　**vessel**「導管、管」　**cardio-respiratory system**「心臓・呼吸器系」

Comprehension check

I. 次の英文が Passage 1 の内容と一致しているなら T (true) を、一致していないなら F (false) を（　）内に記入しなさい。

1. The cells in our muscles need oxygen, glucose and carbon dioxide to work. (　)
2. Oxygen from the air enters the lungs when breathing and then enters the blood. (　)
3. The cardiovascular system transports oxygen, glucose and nutrients to cells and removes waste products. (　)
4. Without enough nutrients, muscles cannot work properly and carbon dioxide and lactic acid increase. (　)
5. Even if endurance athletes work hard, they cannot improve their heart's capability of removing more waste products. (　)

II. 次の英文が Passage 1 の内容と一致するように下記の語群から適切なものを選択し、空欄に記号を記入しなさい。

1. The (　) helps our bodies absorb oxygen from the air.
2. The respiratory system removes (　) from our blood.
3. The (　) is composed of the heart, blood vessels, and blood.
4. Carbon dioxide and (　) are removed from the blood through the cardiovascular system.
5. The harder we exercise, the harder our hearts (　) through the blood vessels to the cells.

a. pump blood	b. carbon dioxide	c. cardiovascular system
d. lactic acid	e. respiratory system	

Passage 2 12

The Kalenjin marathon runners

In recent history there are two nations that dominate long-distance running. They are Kenya and Ethiopia. When we look more closely at the Kenyan athletes, we can see that they come from two **ethnic groups**: the Kalenjin and the **Nandi**. The Kalenjin make up 73% of the Kenyan gold medal winners, but only 10% of the Kenyan population. So, why are the Kalenjin so successful? The main reason is that they come from one region in Kenya, the Rift Valley, which is 2500m above sea level. Running at this **altitude** creates larger lung capacity because there is less oxygen. This means when such athletes run at lower altitude, their lungs are able to provide more oxygen to their muscles. There are other reasons why there are so many Kalenjin marathon runners: children run long distances from an early age, running is seen as a way to escape poverty, and there are many successful **role models** within the community.

注　**Kalenjin**「カレンジン族（ケニア西部やアフリカ大地溝帯付近に居住する民族）」　**ethnic group**「民族グループ」　**Nandi**「ナンディ族（ケニア南西部の高地に居住する民族）」　**altitude**「高度」　**role model**「他人の手本となる人物」

Comprehension check 13

音声を聞いて Passage 2 に関する質問への解答を空欄に３語記入して完成しなさい。

1. What do Kenya and Ethiopia dominate?
   They (　　　　　　　　　　　　　　　　) recently.
2. Why are the Kalenjin successful in long-distance running?
   Because they live in the Rift Valley where the (　　　　　　　　　　　　　　　　).
3. What do Kalenjin children do from a young age?
   They (　　　　　　　　　　　　　　　　).

Derivatives

次の表を完成しなさい。

Verb	Noun
dominate	
supply	
enter	
breathe	
	product

Rearranging

日本語の意味に合うように与えられた単語を使用して文を完成しなさい。

1. water, in, why, human, fish, beings, breathe, cannot, like
   私は人間はどうして魚のように水中で呼吸ができないのか知らない。
   I do not know ( ).
2. to, every, school, the, the, near, park, station, through, day
   私は毎日駅の近くの公園を通って通学していた。
   I went ( ).
3. well, as, of, best, one, known, comic, the, actresses
   その女の人は優れた喜劇女優の一人としてよく知られている。
   The woman is ( ).
4. you, you, get, important, the, more, have, experiences
   年を取れば取るほど、重要な人生経験が多くなる。
   The older ( ) in life.
5. his, age, for, as, thought, healthy, be, of, amazingly
   彼は年の割には驚くほど健康であると考えられる。
   He can ( ).

Unit 5

Physiology IV: Adaption to Aerobic and Anaerobic Exercise

生理学 IV—有酸素と無酸素運動への応用

Vocabulary

次の単語の意味を a ～ e の中から選びなさい。

1. heart rate (   )　　2. anaerobic (   )　　3. fat (   )
4. steady (   )　　5. carbohydrate (   )

a. 脂肪　b. 安定した　c. 心拍　d. 炭水化物　e. 無酸素の

Passage 1

14

When we exercise, our body reacts immediately. Our heart rate speeds up to pump more blood around the body. Also, we breathe harder and faster to supply that blood with more oxygen. There are two types of exercise: **aerobic** (using oxygen) and anaerobic (not using oxygen). Aerobic exercise is not too fast. The heart is able to supply enough oxygen to the muscles. Anaerobic exercise happens in short, fast bursts, so the heart cannot supply enough oxygen to the muscles.

If we start a regular aerobic exercise program, such as going jogging three times a week, our body becomes more efficient. There is **cardio hypertrophy**: this means the heart–the body's engine–becomes larger. Being larger, it can pump more blood around the body. The amount of myoglobin in the slow twitch muscles also increases, so they can supply more oxygen. Aerobic exercise needs a steady source of energy. Our bodies store fats, which can be broken down to release energy. If we exercise regularly, our bodies become better at doing this, so we can lose weight.

When athletes want to increase muscular strength, they often do anaerobic training such as weight training or circuit training. This type of training uses the fast twitch muscles. This exercise causes small **tears** (micro-tears) in the muscles. When the muscles are repaired during recovery, extra protein is added to the muscles. This is known as **muscular hypertrophy**: an increase in muscle size and strength. The skeletal system also becomes stronger as it adapts to the extra forces put on it during the training. Anaerobic exercise uses a lot of energy in a short time. Carbohydrates are simpler than fats. They can release energy very quickly, so are used in anaerobic exercise. Because so much energy is used during anaerobic exercise, it can help people lose weight.

注 **aerobic**「有酸素の、エアロビクスの」 **cardio hypertrophy**「心臓肥大」 **tear**「断裂」 **muscular hypertrophy**「筋肥大」

Comprehension check

I. 次の英文が Passage 1 の内容と一致しているなら T (true) を、一致していないなら F (false) を（ ）内に記入しなさい。

1. When we exercise, our heart pumps more blood to the body. ( )
2. Aerobic exercise is too slow to supply enough oxygen to the muscles. ( )
3. Cardio hypertrophy is a condition in which the heart becomes big. ( )
4. If you want to lose weight, you should do exercise regularly to store energy. ( )
5. Muscular hypertrophy usually occurs as a result of weight training or circuit training. ( )

II. 次の英文が Passage 1 の内容と一致するように下記の語群から適切なものを選択し、空欄に記号を記入しなさい。文頭にくる語も小文字にしてある。

1. When we breathe harder and faster, out ( ) speeds up.
2. ( ) means the heart becomes larger and pumps more blood.
3. The amount of myoglobin in the slow twitch muscles increases in the case of ( ).
4. ( ) is effective to strengthen muscles.
5. When we do anaerobic exercise, ( ) release energy.

a. cardio hypertrophy	b. anaerobic training	c. aerobic exercise
d. carbohydrates	e. heart rate	

Passage 2 15

Sprinting versus long-distance running

If an Olympic sprinter stood next to a marathon runner, what differences would you notice? The sprinter would be taller, with long limbs and much more muscular. The marathon runner would be short and light. That is because their bodies do different jobs. The sprinter needs explosive force for less than ten seconds, while the marathon runner needs to sustain movement over a long time. We can see that the first type is anaerobic exercise, and the second is aerobic. So, is it true that marathon runners do not need to do anaerobic training? Not exactly. There are many benefits a marathon runner can get from anaerobic training. Their bodies can store more glucose (as **glycogen**). Their bodies become better at removing waste products such as lactic acid. Their joints can become stronger, preventing injury. They can also improve their **sprint finishes**.

注　**glycogen**「グリコーゲン（糖原質）」　**sprint finish**「ゴールのラストスパート」

Comprehension check 16

音声を聞いて Passage 2 に関する質問への解答を空欄に３語記入して完成しなさい。

1. What are some differences between a sprinter and a marathon runner?
   A sprinter would be taller and (　　　　　　　　　　) a marathon runner.
2. What benefits does a marathon runner get from anaerobic training?
   He /She can save (　　　　　　　　　　) waste products better.
3. What part of a marathon runner can become stronger after anaerobic training?
   His/Her (　　　　　　　　　　).

Derivatives

次の表を完成しなさい。

Verb	Noun
store	
sustain	
improve	
prevent	
	recovery

Rearranging

日本語の意味に合うように与えられた単語を使用して文を完成しなさい。文頭にくる語も小文字にしてある。

1. feel, comes, when, spring, I
   春がくると新鮮な気分になる。
   (　　　　　　　　　　　　　　　　　　　　　) refreshed.
2. pass, the, studying, he, harder, could
   もっと一生懸命に勉強すれば、彼は試験に合格できるのに。
   (　　　　　　　　　　　　　　　　　　　　　) examination.
3. I, want, English, at, because, be, to, better, speaking
   英語をもっと上手に話したいので練習する。
   I practice (　　　　　　　　　　　　　　　　　　　　　).
4. 1995, been, as, a, known, tourist, since, has, spot
   そこは1995年以来観光地として知られている。
   It (　　　　　　　　　　　　　　　　　　　　　).
5. I, I, seriously, could, get, ill, not, was, up
   とても気分が悪かったので、昨日は起き上がれなかった。
   Because (　　　　　　　　　　　　　　　　　　　　　) yesterday.

Unit 6

Nutrition

栄養

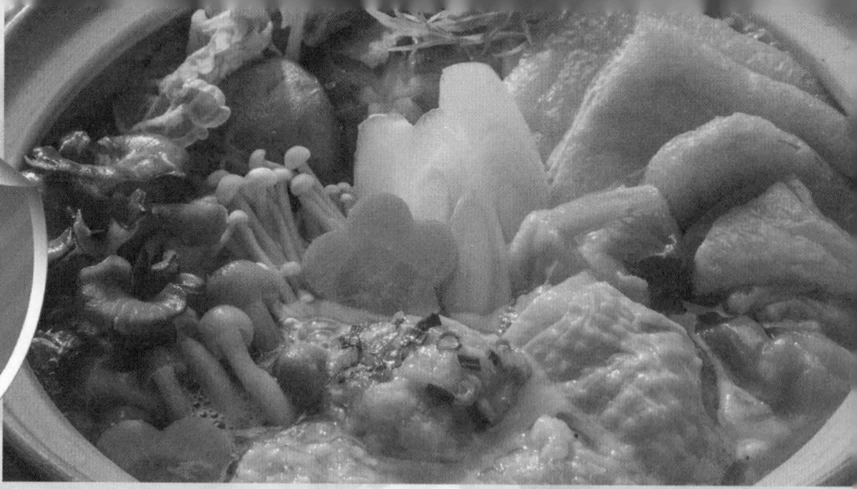

Vocabulary

次の単語の意味を a ～ e の中から選びなさい。

1. recovery (　)　　2. vitamin (　)　　3. replace (　)
4. damage (　)　　5. store (　)

a. ビタミン　b. 蓄える　c. 回復　d. ～の代わりをうめる　e. 損傷

Passage 1

17

“We are what we eat” is a phrase that is often said, and is very true for athletes. What we eat before, during and after training is important. The meal we eat before training will affect the performance, and what is eaten after training affects the recovery.

Nutrients can be separated into **macronutrients**, which provide energy, and **micronutrients**, which do not. Carbohydrates provide energy that can be released quickly. Fats provide energy that is released slowly. Proteins repair muscles and can also provide energy. Micronutrients such as vitamins and **minerals** do not provide energy themselves, but they are needed in energy production.

Hydration is also important. Humans can survive for weeks without food, but only a few days without water. It is important to keep hydrated before, during and after exercise. Other than water, sports drinks are often drunk during and after exercise because they also provide carbohydrates for energy.

Generally speaking, it is important for an athlete to eat a healthy meal balanced with all macro- and micronutrient groups 2~4 hours before training. A meal with different colored fruits and vegetables will provide a variety of vitamins and minerals. Endurance athletes such as long-distance runners may eat a meal with more carbohydrates before a race. They need the carbohydrates to provide energy to their slow twitch muscles that are used at the beginning of the race. Weightlifters, on the other hand, may have a meal with more proteins so that they can repair the damage during training to their fast twitch muscles. Similarly, after training it is important to replace the nutrients that are lost. Endurance athletes will eat more carbohydrates and weightlifters will often drink protein shakes.

Recently the low carbohydrate/high fat diet has become popular in the West. Some endurance athletes are now thinking about using fat for energy, not carbohydrate. The reason is that the human body can store fats longer than carbohydrates. However, this topic needs more research.

注 **macronutrient**「主要栄養素」 **micronutrient**「微量栄養素」 **mineral**「ミネラル」 **hydration**「水分補給」

Comprehension check

I. 次の英文が Passage 1 の内容と一致しているなら T (true) を、一致していないなら F (false) を（ ）内に記入しなさい。

1. If we expect to perform well, we should be careful about the meal we eat before training. ( )
2. Neither carbohydrates nor fat provide energy that is released quickly. ( )
3. Humans can survive without food and water for weeks. ( )
4. The micronutrient group contains vitamins and minerals. ( )
5. The macronutrient group contains carbohydrates and proteins. ( )

II. 次の英文が Passage 1 の内容と一致するように下記の語群から適切なものを選択し、空欄に記号を記入しなさい。文頭にくる語も小文字にしてある。

1. "We are what we eat" means that the ( ) is very important for their performance and recovery.
2. The nutrients which provide energy are ( ).
3. Sports drinks contain water and ( ).
4. ( ) will consume more protein than endurance athletes.
5. Whether ( ) should use fat, not carbohydrate, needs to be researched.

a. meal athletes eat	b. carbohydrates	c. endurance athletes
d. weightlifters	e. macronutrients	

Passage 2 18

A day in the life of a sumo wrestler

People may think that a sumo wrestler's day starts with a large breakfast. This is not true. Sumo wrestlers begin their day with five hours of training in a **fasted state**, without having eaten anything. After training all morning, sumo wrestlers have a large lunch. Although their lunch is high in calories, it is healthy. Typically, wrestlers eat chanko nabe: a hotpot full of seasonal vegetables and **lean** protein, such as chicken, fish or tofu. This is eaten with plenty of rice and pickles. Afternoons are usually spent in recovery. Wrestlers often nap for several hours to help gain weight. After a nap wrestlers do household **chores** before another workout. Another large evening meal is prepared and eaten. Then the sumo wrestlers are free to enjoy their evening relaxing, or watching TV. At 10:30p.m, the lights are turned off so everyone can sleep, before starting the day again at 5:30a.m.

注　**fasted state**「絶食状態」　**lean**「低脂肪の」　**chore**「雑用」

Comprehension check 19

音声を聞いて Passage 2 に関する質問への解答を空欄に３語記入して完成しなさい。

1. What does chanko nabe contain?
   It contains seasonal vegetables and chicken, fish or tofu which
   (　　　　　　　　　　　　　　).
2. Why do sumo wrestlers often take a nap in the afternoon?
   They take a nap (　　　　　　　　　　　　　　).
3. How many hours are sumo wrestlers supposed to sleep at night?
   They are supposed to (　　　　　　　　　　　　　　).

Derivatives

次の表を完成しなさい。

Verb	Noun
	wrestler
	beginning
separate	
replace	
	hydration

Rearranging

日本語の意味に合うように与えられた単語を使用して文を完成しなさい。文頭にくる語も小文字にしてある。

1. we, what, should, at, the, wear, wedding, ceremony, is
   結婚式に何を着るかは非常に重要である。
   ( ) very important.
2. is, to, water, every day, plants, it, necessary, the
   夏には毎日植物に水をやる必要がある。
   ( ) in summer.
3. you, it, speed, important, work, to, for, with, is
   スピードと正確さをもって仕事をすることは重要である。
   ( ) and accuracy.
4. so, the, the, the, hear, TV, that, can, person, on, I, telephone
   電話の声が聞こえるようにテレビを消してください。
   Turn off ( ).
5. heavily, has, after, the, sky, raining
   激しい雨が降った後、空が澄み切った。
   ( ) become clear.

Unit 7

Health and Activity

健康と活動

Vocabulary

次の単語の意味を a ～ e の中から選びなさい。

1. obesity (　　)　　2. fast (　　)　　3. glucose (　　)
4. reduce (　　)　　5. amount (　　)

a. 絶食する　b. 量　c. 減らす　d. 肥満　e. ブドウ糖

Passage 1

20

The Western world is in an obesity crisis. With busy lifestyles people often do not have time to cook properly, so they have to eat **processed food**. This is full of fat, salt and sugar. In other words, there are too many calories in the typical Western **diet**. Technology has made our lives more convenient. That also means that our lives are less active. This combination of over eating and under exercising has resulted in many Western people becoming overweight.

This has led to a new industry—the weight loss industry—and it is huge. In the U.S.A, it was worth $72 billion in 2020. Over the years, popular diets come and go. Low-fat, low-carb, and fasting diets have all been popular over the last ten years. However, people remain overweight. People who diet often end up putting on even more weight when they finish their diet. This is because people often reduce their diet by too many calories: **starving** themselves. When this happens, they reduce the carbohydrate that is stored in their muscles and liver. They also lose water. Glucose from carbohydrates is needed to **metabolize** fat. Without this glucose, the **metabolic rate** of fat slows down. The body now needs to find glucose somewhere. It gets this from muscle. To summarize: a sudden drop in calories does make us lose weight, but first from carbohydrates and water, then from muscle, not from fat. The result is that 95% of all diets are unsuccessful.

So how can we lose weight successfully? The answer is through gentle lifestyle changes. Reduce the amount of food we eat–maybe just by eating on a smaller plate. Start exercising–gently at first. We will notice small changes straight away. As those changes increase, so will the amount of exercise we want to do. Also, we will want to eat healthier food. So put down your smartphone and go out for a walk.

注 **processed food**「加工食品」 **diet**「食事」 **starve**「飢えさせる」 **metabolize**「代謝する」 **metabolic rate**「新陳代謝率」

Comprehension check

I. 次の英文が Passage 1 の内容と一致しているなら T (true) を、一致していないなら F (false) を（ ）内に記入しなさい。

1. The reason for the obesity crisis in the Western world is connected to busy lifestyles. ( )
2. The combination of being overweight and less active results in bad health. ( )
3. The weight loss industry in the U.S.A. always produces successful diets. ( )
4. The reason why most diets are unsuccessful is the sudden drop in calories. ( )
5. We can lose weight through gentle exercise and reducing the amount of food. ( )

II. 次の英文が Passage 1 の内容と一致するように下記の語群から適切なものを選択し、空欄に記号を記入しなさい。

1. People in the Western world are so busy that they have to eat ( ).
2. Because of technology, our lives have become ( ), but we under exercise.
3. People often ( ) through diet to lose weight.
4. Glucose is necessary to ( ) and not to slow down the metabolic rate.
5. If we ( ) gently, we will notice a change and want to do more exercise.

a. starve themselves	b. metabolize fat	c. more convenient
d. start exercising	e. processed food	

Passage 2 21

Metabolic Syndrome

Metabolic Syndrome is a group of conditions that include **high blood pressure**, high blood sugar, high body fat around the waist, and high **cholesterol**. Having one or two of these conditions does not mean you have metabolic syndrome. It means you are at greater risk of having heart disease, a **stroke**, or **type II diabetes** in later life. Metabolic syndrome is caused by unhealthy lifestyle choices. These include poor diet, lack of exercise, drinking and smoking. A change in lifestyle, however, can reverse these conditions. Exercising for over an hour, three times a week is recommended. Also, reducing salt, animal fat and simple carbohydrates (sugars) is advised. So is quitting smoking and cutting down on alcohol. One third of Americans have metabolic syndrome, and the situation is so bad that it has reduced the average **lifespan** in the U.S.A.

注 **metabolic syndrome**「メタボリックシンドローム、代謝症候群」 **high blood pressure**「高血圧」 **cholesterol**「コレストロール」 **stroke**「脳卒中」 **type II diabetes**「2型（生活習慣病タイプの・インスリン非依存性）糖尿病」 **lifespan**「寿命」

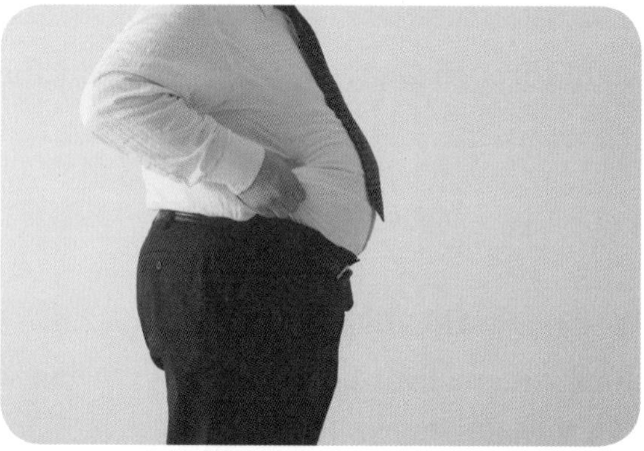

Comprehension check 22

音声を聞いて Passage 2 に関する質問への解答を空欄に3語記入して完成しなさい。

1. What happens if we have high blood pressure and high blood sugar?
   We are (   ) of having heart disease, a stroke, and other conditions in later life.
2. What causes metabolic syndrome?
   Poor diet, (   ), drinking and smoking cause it.
3. How many people have metabolic syndrome in the U.S.A.?
   (   ) them have it.

Derivatives

次の表を完成しなさい。

Verb	Noun
include	
	pressure
	choice
advise	
metabolize	

Rearranging

日本語の意味に合うように与えられた単語を使用して文を完成しなさい。文頭にくる語も小文字にしてある。

1. although, our, more, it, has, lives, made, convenient
   インターネットが生活をより便利にしたが、インターネット上には問題が起きている。
   (　　　　　　　　　　　　　　　　　　　　　　　　　　)
   problems happen on the Internet.
2. led, have, have, the, in, world, foresight, business, us
   実業界で先見の明のある人たちは、私たちを予期せぬ結果に導いてきた。
   People who (　　　　　　　　　　　　　　　　　　　　　　) to
   unexpected results.
3. he, in, because, has, tennis, winning, up, the, game
   彼は練習をより多くしてきたのでテニスの試合では彼の勝利で終わった。
   He ends (　　　　　　　　　　　　　　　　　　) practiced more.
4. year, result, a, lost, is, I, 5kg, that, in
   私は1年で5kg体重を減らしたという結果になった。
   The (　　　　　　　　　　　　　　　　　　　　　　　　).
5. accustomed, to, can, they, people, the, change, lifestyle, are
   慣れたライフスタイルをどうやって人は変えることができるのですか。
   How (　　　　　　　　　　　　　　　　　　　　　　　　)?

Unit 8

Biomechanics I: Newton's Laws

生体力学 I ―ニュートンの法則

Vocabulary

次の単語の意味を a～e の中から選びなさい。

1. physics (　)　　2. analyze (　)　　3. object (　)
4. mass (　)　　5. prevent (　)

a. 質量　b. 妨げる　c. 物理学　d. 分析する　e. 物体

Passage 1

23

Biomechanics is the study of two sciences, physics and **biology**, and analyzes how forces act on the human body to create movement. Through the study of biomechanics athletes can improve their skills and techniques, sport injuries can be prevented, and better equipment and clothing can be designed.

To understand biomechanics, first we must understand Newton's three laws of motion. **Sir Isaac Newton** (1642-1727) was a **physicist** who discovered many of the laws that are the basis of modern biomechanics.

<u>Law of Inertia</u>

Newton's first law says that an object will not move until a larger force makes it move. If we want to pick up a bowling ball, we need a large force to lift it. Similarly, if an object is moving, it will not stop, or change direction, until another force changes it. We can see this as a soccer ball entering a goal is stopped by the net, or changes direction when it is kicked.

<u>Law of Acceleration</u>

Newton's second law says that the acceleration of an object is directly related to the force and **inversely related** to its mass. So a baseball will move faster if it is hit harder. Also, if the baseball were twice as heavy, it would accelerate at half the speed.

<u>Law of Reaction</u>

Newton's third law says that for every **action** there must be an equal and opposite reaction. For example, when we are standing still, gravity pulls us down into the ground. The force of gravity is met by the ground reaction force. With every step a runner takes, there are ground reaction forces that are absorbed by the runner's body. This can cause injury in young runners such as **shin splints**. To prevent such injury running shoes have been designed to absorb some of these forces. Furthermore, the runner's running style may also be making the injury worse. Through close analysis improvements in technique may be suggested.

注 **biology**「生物学」 **Sir Isaac Newton**「サー・アイザック・ニュートン」 **physicist**「物理学者」 **law of inertia**「慣性の法則」 **acceleration**「加速」 **inversely related**「逆相関した」 **reaction**「反作用」 **action**「作用」 **shin splint**「過労性脛部痛」

Comprehension check

I. 次の英文が Passage 1 の内容と一致しているなら T (true) を、一致していないなら F (false) を（ ）内に記入しなさい。

1. Biomechanics is the study of how athletes can be physicians. ( )
2. We can say that Sir Isaac Newton is the father of modern biomechanics. ( )
3. If we want to stop a moving object, another force is needed. ( )
4. As the mass of an object is increased, the acceleration of the object is increased. ( )
5. Running shoes are designed to absorb ground reaction forces. ( )

II. 次の英文が Passage 1 の内容と一致するように下記の語群から適切なものを選択し、空欄に記号を記入しなさい。文頭にくる語も小文字にしてある。

1. The ( ) is helpful for athletes to prevent injuries.
2. Sir Isaac Newton was a physicist and discovered three ( ).
3. ( ) says that an object will not change direction until another force acts upon it.
4. Newton's second law says that the acceleration of an object ( ) the force acting upon the object.
5. According to Newton's third law, there is an ( ) reaction for every action.

a. Newton's first law	b. equal and opposite	c. study of biomechanics
d. laws of motion	e. depends directly upon	

Passage 2 24

The Scientific revolution and the Enlightenment

Sir Isaac Newton lived in interesting times. A scientific revolution was happening in 17th century Europe. During this time, the scientific fields of physics, chemistry, biology, and **astronomy** were born. The modern scientific research method of observing experiments began. Research was published, printed and shared. People worked together developing ideas. The publication of Newton's three laws of motion is now seen as the peak of the scientific revolution. The scientific revolution did not end there, though. The scientific method was applied to society and human behavior, which led to the Enlightenment. Previously, people had relied on religion to explain the meaning of life. However, the scientific method showed that an individual could understand their surroundings through logical and analytical thought. This gave birth to what some people think of as recent ideas: freedom of speech and the individual.

注　**astronomy**「天文学」

Comprehension check 25

音声を聞いて Passage 2 に関する質問への解答を空欄に３語記入して完成しなさい。

1. What interesting times did Sir Isaac Newton live in?
   He lived in the 17th century when ( ) was happening.
2. How did Sir Isaac Newton contribute to modern scientific research?
   He ( ) called Newton's three laws of motion.
3. What had people relied on before the Enlightenment?
   They relied not on the scientific method ( ) explain the meaning of life.

Derivatives

次の表を完成しなさい。

Verb	Noun
develop	
publish	
	enlightenment
explain	
analyze	

Rearranging

日本語の意味に合うように与えられた単語を使用して文を完成しなさい。文頭にくる語も小文字にしてある。

1. how, most, do, know, AI, people, not, translators
   ほとんどの人々は AI 翻訳機がどうやって翻訳するのか知らない。
   (   ) work.
2. understand, customs, different, from, to, to, country, and, manners, are
   国によって風俗習慣が異なることを理解しなくてはならない。
   We have (   ) country.
3. until, with, wait, while, he, a, comes, here, for, his
   彼が娘さんとここにくるまでしばらく待ちましょう。
   Let's (   ) daughter.
4. a, I, do, only, would, not, knew, I, such
   知ってさえいれば、そんなことはしないだろう。
   If (   ) thing.
5. easier, work, and, much, have, technology, made, manual
   科学技術が手作業をずっと容易にしてきた。
   Science (   ).

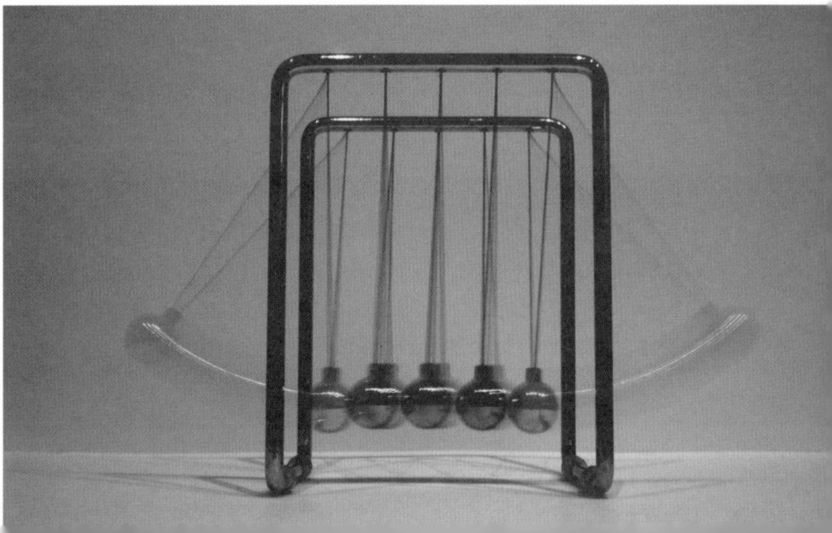

Unit 9

Biomechanics II: Motor Control and Movement

生体力学 II—運動制御と動作

Vocabulary

次の単語の意味を a ～ e の中から選びなさい。

1. complicated (　　)　　2. accurately (　　)　　3. thread (　　)
4. preparation (　　)　　5. plant (　　)

a. 糸　b. 準備　c. 置く　d. 正確に　e. 複雑な

Passage 1

26

Movement is complicated. Muscles need to be told when to contract. These instructions come from the brain and move through the **neurons** along the spine. The neurons in the spine work like a highway. Information is continuously travelling down the spine to the muscles, and back up the spine to the brain. The **senses** in the body, such as sight and touch, are continuously talking with the brain. This is called a feedback loop.

The brain can instruct the body to move very accurately. For instance, we can put the thread through the **eye of a needle**. The brain can also instruct our body to move very quickly. We see this in many sports. However, being both **accurate** and fast is difficult. Athletes who compete in **laser-runs** have to slow down before they can shoot accurately. The relationship between speed and accuracy is known as the speed–accuracy trade-off.

There are different **phases** in movement: preparation, **initiation**, **terminal**, and **follow-through**. In the preparation phase we decide the movement we want to start, or initiate. One example is when a soccer player takes a free kick. First, the player takes a run up. They then plant one foot beside the ball and at the same time they swing back the kicking leg. Planting the foot is important for **accuracy**, so the player watches the ball closely. When the kicking leg is at its highest point, the preparation phase is complete. The next phase is initiation. The player keeps looking at the ball and then releases his kicking leg with **downward** force. The speed of the leg is so fast that there is no time for correction. The terminal phase happens when the foot strikes the ball. At this point the player can make minor changes in the angle to change the direction. The final phase is follow-through. This is important to take a clean shot and to release energy to prevent injury. So how can soccer players place their balls accurately in the net with such power? The answer is practice, practice, practice.

注 **neuron**「神経細胞、ニューロン」 **sense**「感覚」 **eye of a needle**「針の穴」 **accurate**「正確な」 **laser-run**「レーザーラン（レーザーピストルを使用した射撃とランニングを組み合わせた競技）」 **phase**「段階」 **initiation**「開始」 **terminal**「終わり、終わりの」 **follow-through**「フォロースルー、最後まで続けること」 **accuracy**「正確さ」 **downward**「下方に」

Comprehension check

I. 次の英文が Passage 1 の内容と一致しているなら T (true) を、一致していないなら F (false) を（ ）内に記入しなさい。

1. Without our brain we cannot move our body accurately. ( )
2. The brain does not receive any information from the senses in the body. ( )
3. The speed–accuracy trade-off means we have to work quickly. ( )
4. When taking a free kick, a soccer player goes through four phases. ( )
5. If you want to take a clean shot, follow-through is very important. ( )

II. 次の英文が Passage 1 の内容と一致するように下記の語群から適切なものを選択し、空欄に記号を記入しなさい。文頭にくる語も小文字にしてある。

1. Information between the brain and the spine travels through ( ).
2. Without the instruction from ( ) we cannot put a thread through the eye of a needle.
3. ( ) of a free kick is from a player's run up to where his/her kicking leg is at its highest point.
4. At ( ) of a free kick, the player kicks the ball.
5. With practice and practice soccer players ( ).

a. the brain	b. place their balls accurately in the net	c. the neurons in the spine
d. the terminal phase	e. the preparation phase	

Passage 2 27

David Beckham: Soccer player

David Beckham is known all over the world. He probably was not the most naturally talented soccer player. Critics say that in open play he could not dribble the ball very well. What he did do was practice. He used to stay late at the soccer ground when his teammates went home and practice taking free kicks. Beckham himself said: “I must have taken tens of thousands, maybe hundreds of thousands [of free kicks]”. **Practice makes perfect** is a well-known English saying. In David Beckham’s case it was true. With practice, his muscles learned the technique until it became natural. This is called muscle memory. And it meant that he was able to score amazing free kicks in important matches such as the World Cup. Through his efforts, David Beckham became the greatest free kick taker of his time.

注　**Practice makes perfect.**「習うより慣れろ。」

Comprehension check 28

音声を聞いて Passage 2 に関する質問への解答を空欄に３語記入して完成しなさい。

1. What did David Beckham do after his teammates went home?
   He used to stay late and practice (　　　　　　　　　　　　　　　　　).
2. What is muscle memory?
   It means muscles develop a new (　　　　　　　　　　　　　　　　　).
3. Why could David Beckham score free kicks in the World Cup?
   Because he practiced (　　　　　　　　　　　　　　　　　).

Derivatives

次の表を完成しなさい。

Verb	Noun
	memory
	preparation
	initiation
	direction
correct	

Rearranging

日本語の意味に合うように与えられた単語を使用して文を完成しなさい。文頭にくる語も小文字にしてある。

1. you, him, when, know, visit, in, do, to
   東京でいつ彼を訪問すべきか知っていますか？
   ( ) Tokyo?
2. being, being, and, honest, is, one, thing, kind
   正直であることと親切であることは別である。
   ( ) is another.
3. is, friends, between, of, my, I, father, and, like, that
   父と僕との関係は友人関係のようだ。
   The relationship ( ).
4. was, him, keep, on, watching, running, the
   彼がトラックを走り続けるのを見ていた。
   I ( ) track.
5. getting, how, know, could, injured, himself, he, prevent, from
   どうやって彼は怪我を免れることができたか知っていますか？
   Do you ( )?

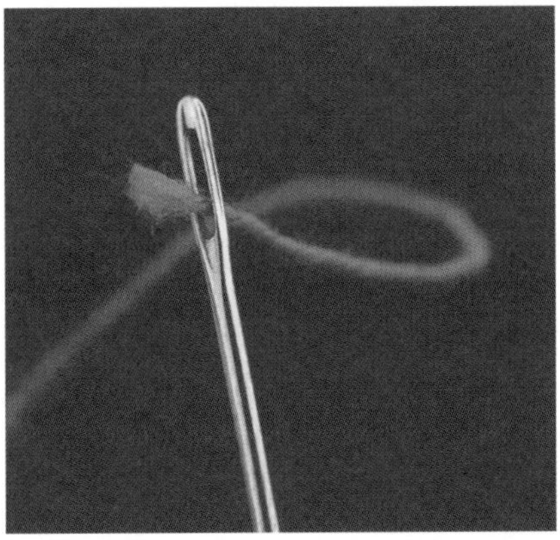

Unit 10

Biomechanics III: Air resistance and aerodynamics

生体力学 III—空気抵抗と空力

Vocabulary

次の単語の意味を a ～ e の中から選びなさい。

1. cause (   )　　2. reduce (   )　　3. teardrop (   )
4. noticeable (   )　　5. sprint (   )

a. 涙のしずく　b. 起こす　c. 全力疾走　d. 顕著な　e. 減らす

Passage 1

29

When an object moves through the air, there is a **frictional force** that tries to stop it. This is **air resistance**. The air in front of the object hits the object before moving around it. As the air moves over the surface, there is more frictional resistance. Finally, when the air meets behind the object, it does not often meet smoothly. This means that the air in front of the object is more dense (higher pressure) than the air behind the object. This air wants to move from high pressure to low pressure, which is the opposite direction that the object is moving. This resistance to movement is known as **drag**.

If you have ever ridden a bicycle on a windy day, you will know how tough it is. A lot of energy must be used, especially if you are cycling directly into the wind. Racing cyclists try to reduce the amount of energy they use by reducing the air resistance. To do this they try to improve their **aerodynamics**. There are several ways of doing this. First, the position of the rider on the bicycle is important. The rider should sit with his head low, so there is less **surface area** to contact the air. Second, the rider's helmet is shaped like a teardrop. This makes sure the air meets smoothly behind the rider's head creating less drag. Finally, the racing cyclist's clothing is made from a special material. This material reduces the **surface friction** caused by moving through the air.

When we watch the team sprint cycling race, two things are noticeable: the cyclists ride close together, and the lead cyclist often changes. Of course, the reason for this is to make the group travel faster. When the three cyclists ride close together, air can pass over the whole group like it were a single object, so there is less total drag. The first cyclist hits the air so they meet the most air resistance. This means they must use more energy to keep the same speed as the other cyclists. Because this makes them tire quickly, after a few **laps** they move to the rear of the group to recover.

注　**frictional force**「摩擦力」　**air resistance**「空気抵抗」　**drag**「抗力」　**aerodynamics**「空力」
surface area「表面積」　**surface friction**「表面摩擦力」　**lap**「走路の一周」

Comprehension check

I. 次の英文が Passage 1 の内容と一致しているなら T (true) を、一致していないなら F (false) を（　）内に記入しなさい。

1. Air resistance is a kind of friction that occurs between air and an object. (　)
2. Drag is a type of force which makes an object move fast through air. (　)
3. Racing cyclists always try to reduce the air resistance by wearing black helmets. (　)
4. Cyclists always try to be in the first position in a team race. (　)
5. If the first cyclist stays at the front of the team, he uses more energy than other members. (　)

II. 次の英文が Passage 1 の内容と一致するように下記の語群から適切なものを選択し、空欄に記号を記入しなさい。

1. When an object moves through air, there is (　) it.
2. If you are cycling directly into the wind, (　) increases.
3. Racing cyclists' clothing uses special materials to (　) friction.
4. The reason why cyclists ride close together is to (　).
5. The first cyclist of a group moves to the rear to (　).

a. resistance to stop	b. reduce the surface	c. recover from tiredness
d. reduce total drag	e. the air resistance	

Passage 2 30

The LZR Racer Swimsuit

In 2008 and 2009, 130 world records in swimming were broken. This was not because the swimmers' ability had improved so much, but was because of a new swimsuit. How could a swimsuit **alter** the results so much? The reason is drag. Moving through water creates 780 times more drag than air. Reducing this drag makes a huge difference in performance. The swimsuit was made with **polyurethane**, which contained bubbles of gas. This made the swimmer float higher in the water, so there was less drag. The material of the swimsuit also pushed water away from its surface. This reduced drag even more. The overall effect of wearing the new **LZR** (pronounced laser) Racer swimsuit was an 8% reduction in drag. And 98% of all medals at the 2008 Beijing Olympics were won by people wearing the suit. The suit was banned in 2010 because it gave wearers an unfair advantage.

注　**LZR**「レーザー（イギリスのSpeedo社が開発した競泳用水着）」　**alter**「変える」　**polyurethane**「ポリウレタン」

Comprehension check 31

音声を聞いてPassage 2に関する質問への解答を空欄に３語記入して完成しなさい。

1. How much bigger is drag in water than in air?
   It is (　　　　　　　　　　) than in air.
2. How did a LZR swimsuit reduce drag in water?
   It contained (　　　　　　　　　　) which made the swimmer float higher.
3. Why was the LZR swimsuit banned in 2010?
   Because it gave wearers (　　　　　　　　　　).

Derivatives

次の表を完成しなさい。

Verb	Noun
improve	
alter	
create	
reduce	
	resistance

Rearranging

日本語の意味に合うように与えられた単語を使用して文を完成しなさい。

1. I, left, umbrella, at, bookstore, before, the, arriving, my
   家に着く前に傘を本屋に忘れたことに気づいた。
   I found (　　　　　　　　　　　　　　　　　　　　　　　　) home.
2. have, ever, be, durian, will, eaten, surprised, at, you, you
   もしドリアンを食べたことがあるなら、その臭いに驚くでしょう。
   If (　　　　　　　　　　　　　　　　　　　　　　　　) its smell.
3. damage, was, caused, the, week, by, typhoon, last
   先週の台風の被害は甚大だった。
   The (　　　　　　　　　　　　　　　　　　　　　　　　) huge.
4. cannot, English, speak, and, French, you, like, do
   あなたのようには英語とフランス語を話すことはできない。
   I (　　　　　　　　　　　　　　　　　　　　　　　　).
5. persuading, on, them, based, in, statistics
   統計に基づいてその理由を説明したので、彼女は彼らを説得することに成功した。
   She succeeded (　　　　　　　　　　　　　　　　　　　　　　　　).

Unit 11

Psychology I: Fixed or Growth Mindset

心理学 I―フィックスト・マインドセットか、グロース・マインドセットか

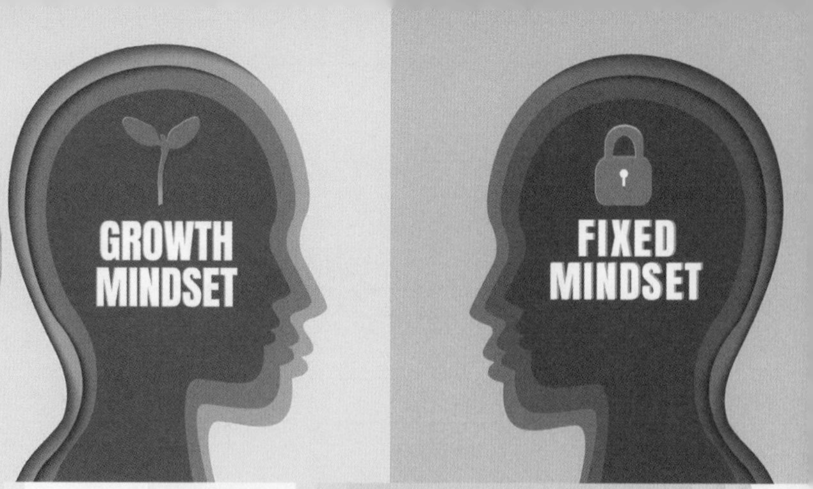

Vocabulary

次の単語の意味を a ～ e の中から選びなさい。

1. physically (　)　　2. lose (　)　　3. talented (　)
4. mentally (　)　　5. limit (　)

a. 負ける　b. 精神的に　c. 肉体的に　d. 限界　e. 才能のある

Passage 1

32

Being an athlete requires more than just being physically fit and training hard. Athletes must also be mentally fit. We have all seen how a team, that was playing well, loses **confidence**. Once the team starts losing, it could lose the match and the next few matches until its confidence returns. Psychology is an important area in sports science.

Let's look at one example. Imagine a group of students are joining a club after entering junior high. When they first practice together, they may notice that some students appear more naturally talented than others. This may be true, but how the team manages that situation is important. There is another way to divide the team: between students with a **fixed mindset** and students with a **growth mindset**. The students who have a fixed mindset believe that natural talent is the most important factor in success. They believe that performance has a limit. However, the students who have a growth mindset believe that they can improve with **effort**: by learning new skills and improving technique.

It is important to understand that this difference in mindset affects students with all levels of ability. Naturally talented students with fixed mindsets may believe that practice is not important. They could feel they are already better than the other students. However, less talented students with growth mindsets may improve quickly with effort and practice. The difference in ability when the students first met does not predict the difference in ability in the future.

Having a growth mindset is not only important in sports. Through hard work and a positive attitude, we can succeed as students and in our careers in the future.

注 **confidence**「自信」 **fixed mindset**「フィックスト・マインドセット」 **growth mindset**「グロース・マインドセット」 **effort**「努力」

Comprehension check

I. 次の英文が Passage 1 の内容と一致しているなら T (true) を、一致していないなら F (false) を（ ）内に記入しなさい。

1. All athletes need to be physically fit and naturally talented. ( )
2. To divide students with different levels of ability is always the best way. ( )
3. The students with a growth mindset believe that performance has a limit. ( )
4. If less talented students have growth mindsets, they may have room for growth. ( )
5. Having a growth mindset and being hard working are important. ( )

II. 次の英文が Passage 1 の内容と一致するように下記の語群から適切なものを選択し、空欄に記号を記入しなさい。

1. Athletes must be both ( ) in addition to training hard.
2. Once an athlete ( ), he/she may continue to lose a match.
3. Students with a ( ) believe that performance has a limit.
4. Students who are ( ) are not promised future good performance.
5. A ( ) is one of the important factors in success.

a. fixed mindset	b. growth mindset	c. mentally and physically fit
d. naturally talented	e. loses confidence	

Passage 2 33

Robert Lewandowski: soccer player

When **Jurgen Klopp**, the Liverpool FC manager was asked who the best player he had ever coached was, he said Robert Lewandowski. And Jurgen Klopp has coached many players, including the Liverpool team who won the Champion's League in 2019. How could he choose Lewandowski from so many wonderful players? The answer is because of Lewandowski's growth. The improvement Lewandowski made since Jurgen Klopp first coached him ten years earlier was remarkable. In 2020 Lewandowski scored the most goals in Europe and won the Champions League with his team, **Bayern Munich**. In the same year he was named UEFAs Men's Player of the Year, beating both **Ronaldo** and **Messi**. Lewandowski achieved all of this through determination and a strong work ethic. Jurgen Klopp joked that because of Lewandowski's amazing improvement, he had helped make Klopp look like a great coach.

注 **Robert Lewandowski**「ロベルト・レヴァンドフスキ（1988年—）ポーランド出身のサッカー選手」 **Jurgen Klopp**「ユルゲン・クロップ（1967年—）ドイツ出身の元サッカー選手で指導者」 **Bayern Munich**「バイエルン・ミュンヘン（ドイツのバイエルン州ミュンヘンを本拠地とする総合スポーツクラブ）」 **Ronaldo**「クリスティアーノ・ロナウド（1985年—）ポルトガル出身のサッカー選手」 **Messi**「リオネル・メッシ（1987年—）アルゼンチン出身のサッカー選手」

Comprehension check 34

音声を聞いて Passage 2 に関する次の質問に対する解答を空欄に３語記入して完成しなさい。

1. Why did Jurgen Klopp choose Robert Lewandowski?
   Because his ( ).
2. What did Lewandowski do in 2020?
   He ( ) goals in Europe and won the Champions League.
3. What made Lewandowski achieve so much?
   He did that through determination and a ( ).

Derivatives

次の表を完成しなさい。

Verb	Noun
achieve	
determine	
	manager
predict	
	growth

Rearranging

日本語の意味に合うように与えられた単語を使用して文を完成しなさい。文頭にくる語も小文字にしてある。

1. being, the, is, of, of, citizen, factors, good, to, a
   善良な市民であることの要素の一つはルールを守ることである。
   One ( ) obey the rules.
2. once, you, you, have, skills, can, narrative
   一旦話術を身につけると、コミュニケーションがうまくいくでしょう。
   ( ) communicate well.
3. restless, interview, appeared, the, before, job
   就職の面接を前にして彼女は落ち着きがないように見えた。
   She ( ).
4. if, a, his, person, works, hard, dream, could, talented
   もし才能のある人が勤勉だったら、夢がかなうだろう。
   ( ) come true.
5. they, a, other, in, than, situation, are, better, people
   彼らは自分たちが他の地域の人々よりいい状況にあることに気づいていない。
   They do not know ( ).

Unit 12

Psychology II: Motivation

心理学 II—動機づけ

Vocabulary

次の単語の意味を a ～ e の中から選びなさい。

1. competition (　)　　2. desire (　)　　3. anxiety (　)
4. stressed (　)　　5. calm (　)

a. 願望　b. ストレスのある　c. 競争　d. 穏やかな　e. 不安

Passage 1

35

"They wanted to win more than us" is often said by soccer coaches after their team lost. This need to win comes from motivation. Motivation has a great effect on competition results. When there are two athletes or teams with similar levels of ability, the most motivated is often the winner.

Motivation can be divided into **intrinsic** and **extrinsic** motivation. Intrinsic comes from inside us. It includes our desire to improve and **beat our personal best**, or our love of the sport. Extrinsic comes from outside of us. It includes money and winning medals or trophies, or making sports fans happy. Athletes should have a combination of both intrinsic and extrinsic motivation. However, intrinsic motivation should be more important. It helps athletes recover from injury, or succeed if their team is **relegated**.

The amount of motivation we have is called **arousal**. When our arousal increases, so does our performance. However, if we have too much arousal our performance can decrease. This is because we may become stressed or have anxiety. It is difficult to perform well like this. Athletes perform at their best when their muscles are relaxed and they feel confident.

All people are different. Some people are shy and other people are outgoing. Outgoing people need high arousal levels to perform well. They perform better in **high-pressure situations**. The opposite is true for shy people. Sports are also different. Some sports need lower arousal levels than others. Let's compare the two individual sports archery and weightlifting. In archery, the athlete needs to be calm and relaxed, so needs low arousal. However, weightlifters need high arousal levels to lift heavy weights. We can see that the arousal level that is needed **depends on** the type of person and the type of sport.

注　**intrinsic**「内部からの」　**extrinsic**「外部からの」　**beat one's personal best**「自己ベストを更新する」　**relegate**「降格させる」　**arousal**「喚起」　**high-pressure situation**「強いプレッシャーの状況」　**depend on**「～による」

Comprehension check

I. 次の英文が Passage 1 の内容と一致しているなら T (true) を、一致していないなら F (false) を（　）内に記入しなさい。

1. "They wanted to win more than us" means motivation is important. (　)
2. If the level of ability is almost the same, the more motivated athlete will win. (　)
3. There are two kinds of motivation: intrinsic and extrinsic. (　)
4. The more arousal we have, the less we can perform. (　)
5. Both shy and outgoing people have the same level of arousal when doing weightlifting and archery. (　)

II. 次の英文が Passage 1 の内容と一致するように下記の語群から適切なものを選択し、空欄に記号を記入しなさい。

1. If two teams have similar levels of ability, the winner is often (　).
2. Extrinsic motivation comes from outside of us such (　).
3. Too much arousal causes (　).
4. Shy people need low arousal levels and perform better in non (　).
5. The necessary (　) the type of sport and person.

a. high-pressure situations	b. as winning medals	c. arousal level depends on
d. more motivated	e. stress or anxiety	

Passage 2 36

Steve Redgrave: 5 times Olympic gold medal rower

The rower **Steve Redgrave** won gold medals at five **consecutive** Olympics. This means he was at the top of his sport for sixteen years. He is undoubtedly a fantastic athlete, but the journey was not easy for him. He had to overcome many difficulties. He is **dyslexic**: this means that he found studying at school very tough. He also had many injuries and illnesses throughout his rowing career, including **diabetes**. He managed to overcome all of these and stay motivated by believing in himself.

"Self-belief is probably the most **crucial** factor in sporting success. The bodies are roughly equal, the training is similar, the techniques can be copied, what separates the achievers is ... not... split times or kilograms. It is the iron in the mind, not the supplements, that wins medals."

Steve Redgrave

注　**Steve Redgrave**「スティーヴ・レッドグレーヴ（1962- ）イングランド・マーロウ出身のボート選手」
consecutive「連続する」　**dyslexic**「失読症の」　**diabetes**「糖尿病」　**crucial**「重要な」

Comprehension check 37

音声を聞いて Passage 2 に関する次の質問に対する解答を空欄に３語記入して完成しなさい。

1. How long had Steve Redgrave been at the top as a rower?
   He had been at the top ( ).
2. How did Steve Redgrave overcome his difficulties?
   He overcame ( ) himself.
3. What serious illness did Steve Redgrave suffer from?
   He ( ).

Derivatives

次の表を完成しなさい。

Verb	Noun
motivate	
	injury
separate	
depend	
include	

Rearranging

日本語の意味に合うように与えられた単語を使用して文を完成しなさい。

1. how, improved, be, can, process, my, thinking, the, of, job
   私は仕事の過程をどのように改善できるかいつも考えている。
   I am always (   ).
2. think, than, humanity, money, important, should, be, more
   人間性は金より当然重要だと思う。
   I (   ).
3. your, your, when, motivated, praises, teacher, performance
   先生にパフォーマンスを褒められたらやる気になりますか。
   Are you (   )?
4. motivated, and, are, are, others, not, some
   会社にはやる気のある者もいるが、そうでない者もいる。
   In our company, (   ).
5. to, try, we, room, clean, keep, the, as, were
   言われたように部屋をきれいにしておくようにしよう。
   Let's (   ) told.

Unit 13
Coaching
コーチング

Vocabulary

次の単語の意味を a ～ e の中から選びなさい。

1. broad (　　)　　2. individual (　　)　　3. tactics (　　)
4. promote (　　)　　5. community (　　)

a. 奨励する　b. 地域　c. 戦術　d. 広い　e. 個人

Passage 1

38

Coaching is one of the many careers in sports science. The roles of the coach are broad. The coach needs to know the rules of the sport they coach. Coaches analyze a team or individual's performance. They then create training programs to improve tactics, skills and techniques, and physical fitness. They also create **strategies** to win competitions.

As sports science has grown, so has the role of the sports coach. In recent years we have learnt that mental health is just as important as physical health. Athletes often need **psychological support**. Although athletes are usually motivated, it can be difficult to keep that motivation. This is true when an athlete is injured, or is not performing well. Top athletes are often only young adults. They need guidance in how to achieve in their sport. Furthermore, they may need **guidance** in life, such as how to manage **finances**, **mass media** or their home lives.

Young adults may not have the healthiest lifestyles. At that age people often stay up late and eat junk food. Previously, after **burning** calories it was thought that they could be **replaced** with any kind of food. We now know this is not true. Improved nutrition improves performance. So coaches try to encourage healthy lifestyles.

Coaches also promote the sport they are involved in. They want to grow their sport. This means they have to manage mass media. This includes things such as interviews after competitions, and an **online presence**. Coaches are also often involved with the community and **charities**.

We can see that coaches must understand many subjects. However, it is not only knowledge that is important. Coaches must be leaders. They must be able to connect to other people. This connection is what makes a difference.

注 **strategy**「戦略」 **psychological support**「心理的支援」 **guidance**「指導、指示」 **finance**「資金管理」 **mass media**「マスメディア」 **burn**「燃焼する」 **replace**「置き替える」 **online presence**「オンラインプレゼンス（インターネット上の存在感）」 **charity**「チャリティ」

Comprehension check

I. 次の英文が Passage 1 の内容と一致しているなら T (true) を、一致していないなら F (false) を（ ）内に記入しなさい。

1. The role of coaching includes the analysis of performance, making programs and strategies, etc. ( )
2. As it is difficult for athletes to keep motivated, they need psychological support from coaches. ( )
3. Top athletes may not be guided in life because their coaches' role is only to make programs. ( )
4. Even though young athletes often eat junk food, they do not need to worry. ( )
5. Coaches manage mass media to promote the sports they are involved in. ( )

II. 次の英文が Passage 1 の内容と一致するように下記の語群から適切なものを選択し、空欄に記号を記入しなさい。

1. The roles of the coach in ( ) are broad.
2. The purpose of ( ) is to improve skills and techniques, etc.
3. To pay attention to ( ) is a role of the sports coach.
4. Coaches try to encourage young top athletes to ( ).
5. Coaches ( ) the community and charities to promote their sports.

a. sports science	b. athletes' mental health	c. are involved with
d. making training programs	e. have a healthy lifestyle	

Passage 2 39

Turning English rugby professional

Clive Woodward was the head coach when English rugby was turning from an amateur sport to a professional sport. He helped improve the England team's fitness, skills and techniques. However, there is a limit to how much training can be done in one day. So, Clive Woodward looked for other areas where the team could be improved. These he called Critical Non-Essentials (CNEs). His idea was that if many small things could be improved by even a small amount, these would all add up to make a difference. One thing he noticed was that the England team often performed worse in the second half of a match. However, this was not a problem of fitness. He then decided to give the players clean rugby **jerseys** at half time. Did changes to CNEs make a difference? Well, England won the Rugby World Cup.

注　**Clive Woodward**「クライヴ・ウッドワード（1956年—）イングランド・ケンブリッジ出身の元ラグビーユニオンプレーヤーおよびコーチ」　**jersey**「ジャージ、（運動選手の着る）セーター」

Comprehension check 40

音声を聞いて Passage 2 に関する次の質問に対する解答を空欄に３語記入して完成しなさい。

1. What did Clive Woodward help the English team improve?
   He helped it improve fitness, ( ).
2. What are the effects of Critical Non-Essentials?
   Even if a limited number of small things is improved, it ( ).
3. What was one of the reasons why the England team often performed worse in the second half of a match?
   It was not a problem of fitness but ( ).

Derivatives

次の表を完成しなさい。

Verb	Noun
	guidance
achieve	
involve	
	presence
	knowledge

Rearranging

日本語の意味に合うように与えられた単語を使用して文を完成しなさい。

1. you, to, enter, know, going, corporate, the, are, culture
入社する会社の社風を知るべきだ。
You should ( ).

2. my, as, as, a, breakfast, for, big, lunch, health
私は健康のために昼食と同じくらいたっぷり朝食を食べる。
I eat ( ).

3. was, journey, thought, from, that, he, his, come, would, back
彼は旅行からすぐ戻ると思われていた。
It ( ) soon.

4. most, of, me, her, that, lack, experience, surprised
私を多いに驚かせたのは彼女の経験不足だった。
It was ( ).

5. happen, is, know, there, to, to, what, about
私はそこでまさに起きようとしていることを知りたい。
I would like ( ).

Unit 14

Sports Sociology

スポーツ社会学

Vocabulary

次の単語の意味を a ～ e の中から選びなさい。

1. belief (　) 2. conservative (　) 3. politics (　)
4. opportunity (　) 5. advertise (　)

a. 保守的な　b. 機会　c. 宣伝する　d. 政治　e. 信念

Passage 1

41

Sport sociology is the study of sport and society. It looks at how sports affect **cultural values** and beliefs. Through sport, we learn about fair play, the reward of working hard and never giving up. We learn how to work in a team, and how important rules are. All of these are important lessons for how to be a good member of society. Sport sociology also teaches us the opposite **relationship**: how cultural values and beliefs affect sport. Let's compare two great **national sporting events**: Wimbledon in the U.K. and the Super Bowl in the U.S. Wimbledon is traditional and conservative. The atmosphere is quiet and the tennis players all wear white. The atmosphere at the Super Bowl is more like a rock concert. There are many **commercial breaks** and also a half time show, which has live performances from popular artists. These sporting events show the culture of their individual countries.

Sport sociology also examines the relationship between sport and important things in life such as the economy, politics, and the media. We can see how all these things are connected when we look at soccer. Like many things in life, soccer is controlled by money. A top player is paid a huge salary by their team and can also make more money by being **sponsored** by sporting brands. **Corporations** sponsor teams and events such as the World Cup. The World Cup is the largest sporting event in the world and costs billions of dollars to host, and also billions of dollars for the **TV rights**. Because it is watched by more people than the Olympics, the opportunity to have their brand seen by billions of people means corporations will pay a lot of money to advertise there.

Sport sociology is also connected to issues that affect our lives like gender, religion and race. As in the business world, male soccer players are paid much more than women. After **scoring a goal**, Muslim soccer players often pray to their God, and Christian soccer players may make the sign of a cross. Finally, **racial abuse** can still be heard from soccer supporters, and because of this, matches have been stopped.

注 **cultural values**「文化的価値観」 **relationship**「関係」 **national sporting event**「国家的なスポーツイベント」 **commercial break**「コマーシャルのための中断」 **sponsor**「スポンサーになる」 **corporation**「企業」 **TV rights**「TV 放映権」 **score a goal**「ゴールを決める」 **racial abuse**「人種差別的発言、人種差別」

Comprehension check

I. 次の英文が Passage 1 の内容と一致しているなら T(true) を、一致していないなら F(false) を（　）内に記入しなさい。

1. Sport sociology teaches the reward of working hard and fair play. (　)
2. Wimbledon in the U.K. and the Super Bowl in the U.S. are good examples of how each culture is different. (　)
3. Sport sociology has no connection to politics. (　)
4. Corporations will pay more money for the World Cup than a small event such as sumo. (　)
5. As male and female players are paid equally, there is no gender problem in the sport world. (　)

II. 次の英文が Passage 1 の内容と一致するように下記の語群から適切なものを選択し、空欄に記号を記入しなさい。文頭にくる語も小文字にしてある。

1. Sport sociology studies how sports affect (　).
2. What we learn through sport is useful to be (　).
3. While the atmosphere at Wimbledon is (　), the Super Bowl is not.
4. We can see how (　) are connected when we look at soccer.
5. (　) from soccer supporters can stop matches.

a. traditional and conservative	b. racial abuse heard
c. the economy, politics, and the media	d. cultural values and beliefs
e. a good member of society	

Passage 2 42

Soccer hooliganism

Sport has without doubt had a positive influence on society. Some of our best memories are of sports day at elementary school, or belonging to a club in junior high. Sport teaches us many valuable lessons that we can apply to our lives. However, there is a dark side to sport. With so much money involved, there is **corruption**, **match fixing**, and **drug cheating**. But money is not the cause of all of sports problems. Money does not cause soccer hooliganism. Most soccer supporters are young, male and working class. They support their local team with fierce pride. Unfortunately, when groups of young males consume large amounts of alcohol, this pride can turn to violence, especially if the other team is a local rival.

注　**hooliganism**「乱暴、暴動」　**corruption**「堕落、贈収賄」　**match fixing**「八百長」　**drug cheating**「薬物不正使用」

Comprehension check 43

音声を聞いてPassage 2に関する次の質問に対する解答を空欄に３語記入して完成しなさい。

1. What positive memories of sports do we have?
   They may be (　　　　　　　　　　) elementary school, or belonging to a club in junior high.
2. What valuable lessons about life do we learn through sport?
   We learn (　　　　　　　　　　) as a team, the importance of effort, and the rewards of success.
3. When can soccer supporters' pride turn to violence?
   It can turn to violence when they (　　　　　　　　　　) of alcohol.

Derivatives

次の表を完成しなさい。

Verb	Noun
	corruption
consume	
	belief
compare	
connect	

Rearranging

日本語の意味に合うように与えられた単語を使用して文を完成しなさい。文頭にくる語も小文字にしてある。

1. my, guitar, to, how, play, the, since, learning, been
   高校生時代からギターの弾き方を習っている。
   I have (　　　　　　　　　　　　　　　　　　　　　　) high school days.
2. to, university, learned, what, we, we, at, can, apply
   大学で学んだことは人生に応用できる。
   (　　　　　　　　　　　　　　　　　　　　　　　　　　) our lives.
3. we, the, thing, bird, looked, was, a, little, when
   それをよく見ると小鳥だとわかった。
   We found (　　　　　　　　　　　　　　　　　　　　　　) closely.
4. a, language, will, to, view, learn, foreign, your, broaden
   外国語を学ぶ機会はあなたの視野を広げるでしょう。
   The opportunity (　　　　　　　　　　　　　　　　　　　　).
5. one, is, sports, connected, events, to, as, of
   私たちの会社はスポンサーの一つとしてスポーツイベントに関係している。
   Our company (　　　　　　　　　　　　　　　　　　　　) the sponsors.

Unit 15

Review

復習

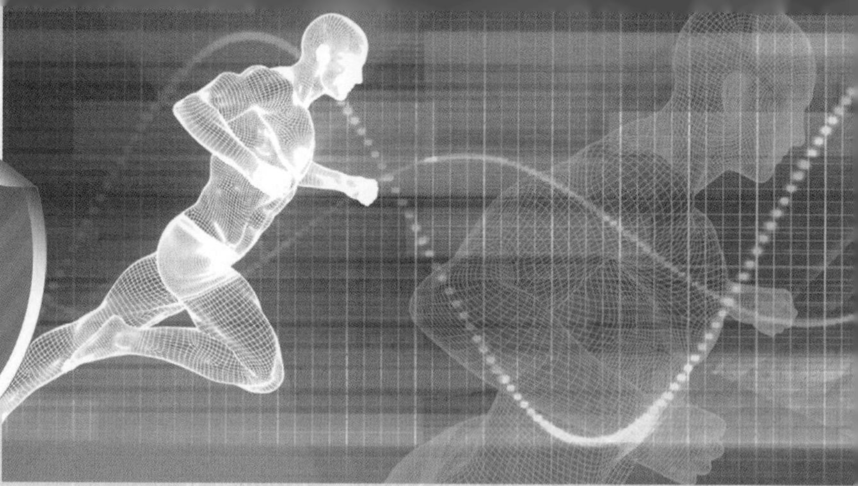

I. 左側の科学用語を説明したものを右側から選び、記号で答えなさい。

1. biology ( )	a. the study of how objects, forces, and energy act on each other
2. biomechanics ( )	b. the study of how humans behave in groups
3. nutrition ( )	c. the study of how humans think, feel, and behave
4. physics ( )	d. the study of food and how it works in the body
5. physiology ( )	e. the study of how living things stay alive
6. psychology ( )	f. the study of living things
7. sociology ( )	g. the study of the structure and movement of living things

II. 二人の科学者、ニュートンとマトヴェーエフに関する文を読み、ニュートンのことならNをマトヴェーエフのことならMを（　）内に記入しなさい。（8ページと36ページ参照）

1. He was a physiologist. ( )
2. He was at the birth of modern scientific research. ( )
3. He was a physicist. ( )
4. His methods helped athletes win Olympic medals. ( )
5. He was from the United Kingdom. ( )
6. He was from the Soviet Union. ( )
7. He invented modern periodization. ( )
8. He discovered three laws of motion. ( )

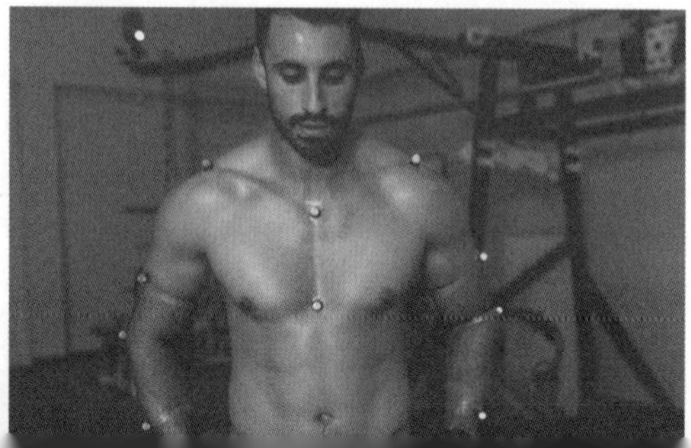

III. 次の英文を読み、下線部に入る科学用語を記入しなさい。

ヒント：反対の意味の科学用語はボールド体で強調してある。

1. When we breathe in, **oxygen** enters our blood, and when we breathe out ________________ leaves.
2. There are two types of exercise: **aerobic** uses oxygen and ________________ does not.
3. People with a **fixed mindset** believe that natural talent is the most important factor. However, people with a ________________ believe all people can improve with effort.
4. **Intrinsic** motivation comes from inside us, while ________________ motivation comes from outside us.
5. Slow twitch muscle fibers are used for **endurance** tasks, and fast twitch fibers are used for ________________ or power.
6. Nutrients can be separated into **macronutrients** which provide energy, and ________________ that do not.
7. Both **carbohydrate** and ________________ provide energy. **Carbohydrates** release energy quickly, while ________________ release energy slowly.
8. The **speed**- ________________ trade-off shows our brains can either do things quickly but with mistakes, or slowly with fewer mistakes.

IV. 左側の科学用語の意味を右側から選び、記号で答えなさい。

1. aerodynamics (　)	a. 重力
2. cardiovascular system (　)	b. グリコーゲン
3. diabetes (　)	c. 呼吸器系
4. force of gravity (　)	d. 空力
5. ground reaction force (　)	e. 地面反力
6. glycogen (　)	f. 慣性の法則
7. hypertrophy (　)	g. 循環器系
8. law of inertia (　)	h. 脊椎
9. motor control (　)	i. ミオグロビン
10. myoglobin (　)	j. 糖尿病
11. respiratory system (　)	k. 運動制御
12. vertebra (　)	l. 肥大

V. 次の英文の空欄に最も適した単語を記入しなさい

1. (   ) the science of sport has grown, so have the career-related fields.
2. Bones have places (   ) muscles can attach.
3. Fast twitch muscles are twice as big (   ) slow twitch muscles.
4. (   ) the muscles do not get enough nutrients, waste products increase and cause fatigue.
5. Adding protein to muscles is known (   ) muscular hypertrophy.
6. Other (   ) water, sports drinks are often drunk during and after exercise.

VI. 次の与えられた動詞を適当な形に変えて文中の（　）内に記入しなさい。

1. Even though the team (   ) less talent, they were able to beat the other team. (have)
2. Fraser is known as one of the fittest men in the world, (   ) the CrossFit Games every time from 2016 to 2020. (win)
3. If we exercise regularly, our bodies become better at (   ) this. (do)
4. When the muscles (   ) during recovery, extra protein is added to the muscles. (repair)
5. There (   ) many benefits a marathon runner can get from anaerobic training. (be)

Image Credits
All photographs © Shutterstock.com except:
p.40 ©Alexander Gordeyev / Shutterstock.com

An Introduction to Sports Science in English [B-953]
英語で学ぶスポーツ科学

1 刷 2023年1月26日

著 者 ジュリアン・ナット Julyan Nutt
倉橋 洋子 Yoko Kurahashi
山本 伸 Shin Yamamoto

発行者 南雲一範 Kazunori Nagumo
発行所 株式会社 南雲堂
〒162-0801 東京都新宿区山吹町361
NAN'UN-DO Co., Ltd.
361 Yamabuki-cho, Shinjuku-ku, Tokyo 162-0801, Japan
振替口座：00160-0-46863
TEL: 03-3268-2311（営業部：学校関係）
03-3268-2384（営業部：書店関係）
03-3268-2387（編集部）
FAX: 03-3269-2486

編集者 加藤 敦
表 紙 Nスタジオ
組 版 Office haru
検 印 省 略
コード ISBN978-4-523-17953-5 C0082

Printed in Japan

E-mail nanundo@post.email.ne.jp
URL https://www.nanun-do.co.jp/